My Family Reunion

Learning to Recognize Fractions as Part of a Group

Christine Clement

Rosen Classroom Books & Materials
New York

Published in 2004 by The Rosen Publishing Group, Inc.
29 East 21st Street, New York, NY 10010

Book Design: Haley Wilson

Photo Credits: Cover © Bill Bachmann/Index Stock; pp. 4, 6 © Ariel Skelley/Corbis; p. 9 ©
Raeanne Rubenstein/Index Stock; p. 10 © George Shelley/Corbis; p. 12 © ThinkStock LLC/Index Stock;
p. 14 © Jeff Greenberg/Index Stock.

ISBN: 0-8239-8923-2
6-pack ISBN: 0-8239-7451-0

Manufactured in the United States of America

Contents

Does your family ever have special parties?
Family reunions are a lot of fun!

A Family Reunion

I have a very big family. Some people in my family live close by, and I get to see them often. Other people in my family live far away, so I do not see them as much. Every year, we have a family **reunion** (ree-YOON-yuhn) so that we can all spend time together. It is always fun to see everyone!

Softball is a lot like baseball, but it is played
with a larger, softer ball.

A Party in the Park

     We have our family reunion at a different person's house each year. First, everyone eats together. Then we go to a park to play games. My favorite game is **softball**. This year, 7 of us play softball. Two of the 7 players are wearing red shirts. We can use **fractions** to see what part of the group that is!

> 2 of the 7 softball players are wearing red shirts.
>
> **2 out of 7 =** $\dfrac{2}{7}$

A Game of Tennis

Some people in my family like to play **tennis**. A game of tennis can be played by 2 people or by 4 people. This year, 4 people want to play tennis. Three of the 4 players are wearing white shirts. What fraction of the group is wearing white shirts?

3 of the 4 players are wearing white shirts.

3 out of 4 = $\frac{3}{4}$

If 2 people play tennis, the game is called "singles." If 4 people play tennis, the game is called "doubles."

Horseshoes is played by throwing horseshoes at a stake in the ground. Players win points by getting the horseshoes close to or around the stake.

Let's Play Horseshoes!

Some people in my family like to play horseshoes. This year, 4 people want to play horseshoes. One of the 4 players brings her own horseshoes from home. What fraction of the group brings their own horseshoes?

1 of the 4 players brings horseshoes from home.

1 out of 4 = $\frac{1}{4}$

Do you like to play cards? What is your
favorite card game?

A Game of Cards

Some people in my family like to play cards. This year, 2 people want to play cards. One of the 2 players wants to go swimming later in the day. What fraction of the group will go swimming after the card game is over?

1 of the 2 players will go swimming later in the day.

1 out of 2 = $\frac{1}{2}$

At the Pool

Some people in my family like to go swimming. This year, 3 people want to go swimming at the park's pool. One of the 3 swimmers brings snacks to the pool. What fraction of the group brings snacks to the pool?

1 of the 3 swimmers brings snacks to the pool.

1 out of 3 = $\frac{1}{3}$

Glossary

fraction (FRAK-shun) One or more of the equal parts that make up a whole number, group, or thing.

reunion (ree-YOON-yuhn) The act of coming together again after having been apart.

softball (SOFT-ball) A game that is like baseball, but played on a smaller field with a larger, softer ball.

tennis (TEH-nuhs) A game played by two or four players on a special court. Players use rackets to hit a ball back and forth over a net.

Index